Symbols of Freedom

The Statue of Liberty

Tristan Boyer Binns

Heinemann Library
Chicago, Illinois

Designed by Lisa Buckley
Printed in China

06 05
10 9 8 7 6 5 4

Library of Congress Cataloging-in-Publication Data
Binns, Tristan Boyer, 1968-
       The Statue of Liberty / Tristan Boyer Binns.
          p. cm. -- (Symbols of freedom)
       Includes bibliographical references (p.) and index
       ISBN 1-58810-121-5 (lib. bdg.)   ISBN 1-58810-405-2 (pbk. bdg.)
          1. Statue of Liberty (New York, N.Y.)--Juvenile literature. 2. New York
       (N.Y.)--Buildings, structures, etc.--Juvenile literature. [1. Statue of Liberty (New York,
       N.Y.) 2. National monuments. 3. New York (N.Y.)--Buildings, structures, etc.] I. Title.

F128.64.L6 B53 2001
974.7'1--dc21
                                                                                    00-058144

Acknowledgments
The author and publishers are grateful to the following for permission to reproduce copyright material: p.4, 7 Michael S. Yamashita/Corbis, p.5 Currier and Ives/PictureQuest, p.6 Charles Rotkin/Corbis, p.8 Archive Photos/ PictureQuest, p.9, 18, 19, 24, 25 Library of Congress, p.10 Todd Gipstein/Corbis, p.11 Gail Mooney/Corbis, p.12 Philip Gould/Corbis, p.13 Susan Ragan/AP Photo, p.14, 15 Corbis, p.16 Cooper-Hewitt National Design Museum, Smithsonian, p. 17, 20, 23 Bettemann/Corbis, p.21 AP Photo/AIP, p.22 Museum of the City of New York/Corbis, p.26 Robert Maass/Corbis, p.27 Joseph Sohm/ChromoSohm/Corbis, p.28 Larry Lee Photography/Corbis, p.29 Picture Colour Library Ltd./eStock/PictureQuest.
Cover photograph by Picture Colour Library Ltd./eStock Photography/PictureQuest.

Every effort has been made to contact copyright holders of any material reproduced in this book. Any omissions will be rectified in subsequent printings if notice is given to the publisher.

Some words are shown in bold, **like this.**
You can find out what they mean by looking in the glossary.

Contents

The Statue of **Liberty** is a sculpture of a lady holding a **torch.** It stands on Liberty Island outside New York City. It looks out to sea.

The Statue of Liberty is a **symbol** of the freedom that Americans enjoy. It was a present from France. It has been standing for more than 100 years.

Big Idea

The Statue of **Liberty** is one of the biggest statues ever made. It is as tall as an office building. It weighs almost as much as 45 elephants!

The statue wears a crown with seven spikes.
The **torch** is in her right hand. She holds a
tablet in her left arm.

Thinking About Freedom

The Statue of **Liberty** has been an important **symbol** of freedom to **immigrants.** For many people, the statue has meant hope for a better life.

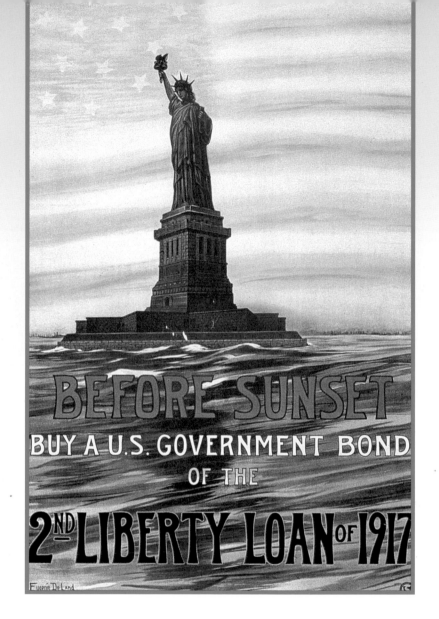

The Statue of Liberty also stands for a strong United States. During war times, pictures of the statue have been used to ask people to give money.

People come from all over the world to visit the Statue of **Liberty.** They take a **ferry** from New York City to Liberty Island.

Visitors go into the statue through the **pedestal.**
There are stairs inside. People can go up to a
balcony at the top of the pedestal.

There are stairs inside the Statue of **Liberty,** too. People can climb up to the crown. No one can go into the **torch.**

12

There are windows in the crown. Visitors can see far out over New York City and New York **Harbor.**

The French Idea

The idea for the statue started more than 100 years ago. The **Civil War** had come to an end. Two men from France wanted to celebrate.

Frédéric Bartholdi was one of the men. He was famous for making big statues. He came to the United States to talk about his idea.

Raising Money

Bartholdi said that France would pay for the statue. The United States would pay for the **pedestal.** People liked this idea. They said they would help raise money.

To help raise money, Bartholdi made the statue's right arm and the **torch.** He sent them to a fair in Philadelphia. People paid money to go inside them.

Building Liberty

The statue was built in Paris, France.
Bartholdi's design was made into giant **molds.**
Workers hammered sheets of **copper** into the
molds to make the shape of the statue.

The **hollow** copper statue was attached
to a frame. The frame was made of **iron,** so
that the whole statue would be strong.

It took almost ten years to make the statue. Then it was taken apart! The statue was packed into 214 crates and sent to New York by boat.

The statue arrived in June 1885. One year later, the **pedestal** was finished. The statue was placed on the pedestal.

The statue was **dedicated** on October 28, 1886. The weather was cold and wet. Even so, crowds of people came to see the parades and the celebration.

A French flag covered the statue's face.
President Grover Cleveland made a speech.
Then **Bartholdi** took down the French flag.
People saw the statue's beautiful face for the
first time.

23

Big Changes

Time and weather hurt the Statue of **Liberty.**
By 1980, she needed a lot of repairs. France
and the United States worked together to
plan the hard work.

Rusted **iron** bars were taken out. New bars were made from **stainless steel.** The statue was cleaned inside and out. The old **torch** was taken down. A new one was made.

Happy Birthday!

It took two years to repair the statue.
Better stairs and elevators were put inside.
The repairs cost 87 million dollars.

The work was finished in time for July 4, 1986. There was a huge party. Fireworks lit up the sky. It was the Statue of **Liberty's** 100th birthday!

Liberty Lighthouse

The outside of the Statue of **Liberty** is made of **copper.** When the statue was new, it looked like a new penny. But copper turns green from the air and weather.

The Statue of Liberty was built to be a **lighthouse.** The first lights were in the statue's crown. Then the **torch** was made into a huge lamp. The new torch does not light up from inside.

Statue of Liberty

★ Each of the statue's fingernails is bigger than this book.

★ Forty people can fit in the statue's head.

★ The statue's mouth is as wide as a table.

★ There are 25 windows in the crown.

★ July 4, 1776 is written on the **tablet.** That is the date the United States became **independent** from Britain.

★ A broken chain lies at the statue's feet. It shows that people must be free.

Glossary

balcony upstairs porch or walkway

Bartholdi, Frédéric French sculptor who lived from 1834 to 1904

Civil War U.S. war in the 1800s, in which northern states fought against southern states

copper soft, reddish-brown metal that is easy to shape

dedicated opened for the public

ferry large boat that carries people and sometimes cars from the land to an island

harbor place where ships can stay safe from storms

hollow empty inside

immigrant person who comes from another country to make a home in a new country

independent not ruled or controlled by another country

iron strong metal that can be made into different shapes when it is hot or melted

liberty freedom to choose your work, your religion, and your friends

lighthouse tower with a bright light at the top that helps ships find their way in storms or fog

mold empty container that is made into a shape and then has hot liquid poured inside it to form something else

pedestal base that a statue stands on

stainless steel mixture of metals that cannot rust

symbol something that stands for an idea

tablet flat piece of stone with writing on it

torch flaming light that a person carries

More Books to Read

An older reader can help you with these books:

Doherty, Craig A. *The Statue of Liberty*. Woodbridge, Conn.: Blackbirch, 1996.

Quiri, Patricia R. *The Statue of Liberty*. Danbury, Conn.: Children's Press, 1998.

Strazzabosco-Hayn, Gina. *The Statue of Liberty*. New York: Rosen Publishing Group, 1997.

Index